MAKING HISTO

EDUCATION

KT-425-441

COLUMBUS
and the NEW
WORLD

Written by
Fiona Clarke

Illustrated by
Mark Bergin

(s)

910.9

S316630

2100038737

E.L.R.S.

SIMON & SCHUSTER
YOUNG BOOKS

Contents

Design   David Salariya
Editor   Penny Clarke

First published in Italy by
Giunti Gruppo Editoriale, Firenze
under the title NEL NUOVO MONDO CON
CRISTOFORD COLOMBO

This edition first published in 1993 by
Simon & Schuster Young Books
Campus 400
Maylands Avenue
Hemel Hempstead
Herts HP2 7EZ

© 1990 by Giunti Gruppo Editoriale
English version © 1993 by
Simon & Schuster Young Books

ISBN 0 7500 1351 6 (hardback)
ISBN 0 7500 1352 4 (paperback)

Printed in Italy by Giunti Industrie Grafiche

Introduction

THIS BOOK TELLS THE STORY of Christopher Columbus who was born in Italy in 1451 and died in Spain in 1506. Today, Columbus is remembered as the first man to show it was possible to sail across the Atlantic Ocean. In doing this he discovered a whole 'New World' – the continent of North and South America.

In fact, Viking sailors probably sailed across the icy waters of the northern Atlantic, from Greenland to Vinland on the North American coast, many hundreds of years before. But, by Columbus's time, these Vikings and their adventures had long been forgotten. It has been suggested recently that Portuguese explorers crossed the Atlantic about forty years before Columbus, but that they did not survive to return to Europe, so nobody knew about their discovery.

Columbus lived at a time when many merchants and adventurers were looking for new routes to travel from Europe to the rich lands in the east. The Turks had closed the old, eastward, overland trade routes to India and China. Some explorers searched for new ways to travel to the east by sea. Bartholomew Dias, for example, pioneered a shipping route to India around the southernmost tip of Africa in 1488.

Columbus, however, had other ideas. Fascinated by the tales he heard sailors telling in the ports of Spain and Portugal, he became convinced that he would be able to reach the fabulous civilizations of China and Japan by travelling westwards. Although he studied maps and charts (sea maps), there were none that could help him on his epic voyage. As a result, when he did reach land he did not realize – and nor did anyone else at the time – that the whole vast continent of North and South America lay between Europe and his destination.

Today, thanks to television and photography, we know what places look like – including the surface of the moon! But Columbus and his men had no such knowledge. They really were sailing into the unknown.

The Making of an Explorer

CHRISTOPHER COLUMBUS WAS BORN IN 1451 in Genoa, a bustling port in northern Italy. At first his father worked as a weaver, later he ran an inn. Columbus's family were not well off and neither he nor his brothers went to school. No-one knows who taught him to read and write, to do simple mathematics or to draw maps, but, by the time he was a young man, Columbus could do all these things – all of them essential for anyone who was going to be an explorer.

Ports are busy, noisy and exciting places and fifteenth-century Genoa was no exception. Although we cannot be certain, Columbus and his friends probably hung about the port area, watching the activity around the great sailing ships as they were loaded and unloaded at the quayside. They may even have run errands for the sailors to earn a little money or the chance to sneak aboard and have a look round.

Perhaps it was the excitement of seeing the ships and their cargoes and hearing tales of the far-off lands they visited, that made Columbus decide to become a sailor and explorer. Of course we cannot be sure about this, but we do know that by the time he was in his early teens Columbus had left home. He was finding work on small ships trading along the Italian coast. Columbus's life at sea had begun.

▷ The streets of Genoa were crowded and busy. They were also noisy. The stallholders shouted their wares, describing what was best and fresh that day. Beggars (there's one beside the doorway with the tiled porch) called out asking people to give them money or food. The iron rims of cartwheels made a terrible clatter as they bumped over the uneven stones paving the streets. Hens squawked and cackled as they were carried in wicker baskets slung from poles, and because it was a port, the harsh calls of the seagulls rose above everything.

A Wealthy Trade Centre

GENOA WAS AN IMPORTANT TRADING centre, specializing in goods from the Far East. The city's merchants had grown rich selling furs from Russia, silks from China, jewellery from Iran and spices from India and south-east Asia.

These goods reached Genoa after long, dangerous journeys. First they were carried through hostile country by packhorse or camel train to Genoese trading posts on the coast of the Black Sea or the great city of Constantinople, on the north-east shore of the Mediterranean. Then they were loaded onto Genoese ships bound for Italy. Often the ships were attacked by pirates from North Africa or by warships belonging to Genoa's great rival, the city of Venice.

All the risks were worth it, however, until, in 1453, disaster struck. Constantinople was captured by the Turks, who took control of all the Black Sea trading posts, and all the overland routes to the east. They sent warships to attack any Genoese boat that ventured into the eastern Mediterranean.

The result of these actions by the Turks was disastrous for the people of Genoa. The Turks now controlled all the trade routes the Genoese merchants had worked so hard to build up, and the trade that had brought riches to them would bring riches to the Turks.

▷ At the entrance to Genoa's harbour was a lighthouse, a welcome sight at the end of a voyage! When the ship tied up at the quayside there was lots to do. The cargo had to be unloaded and checked. Then the ship itself had to be inspected to make sure it had suffered no damage – winter storms in the Mediterranean can be very severe. The sails and all the ropes of the rigging had to be checked. A frayed rope can easily break in a strong wind and a broken rope could lead to a broken mast and the end of a voyage.

Early Days at Sea

TO MAKE UP FOR THEIR lost trade with the east, the Genoese merchants increased their trade with the rest of Europe. Smaller ships called at the ports along the Mediterranean coasts of France and Spain. Larger ones sailed out of the Mediterranean through the Straits of Gibraltar and into stormier seas on their way north to France, England and Germany.

Columbus probably sailed in one of these ships, working as a messenger for his father and other businessmen. He would take orders and try to win more business in the ports at which the ship called. Although today Columbus is remembered as a great sailor, he never actually worked as one! But, because he had always been interested in ships and the sea, he would have learnt a great deal on these voyages, just by watching the captains and crews at work.

In 1474 or 1475, when he was about 23, Columbus went as a trader to the island of Chios, which belonged to Genoa. This island (modern Kos) is just off the Turkish mainland, and the people of the island paid the Turks a large sum of money each year to stop them attacking the island and the ships sailing to and from it. Encouraged by a successful year on Chios, Columbus returned to Genoa, where he set up in business as a trader and traveller.

Soon after this, on a Genoese trading expedition to England, Columbus nearly lost his life. Just off the Portuguese coast, the ship he was sailing in was attacked by French pirates. The Genoese sailors tried to set fire to the pirate ships, but the wind blew the flames back onto their own ships. Columbus's one hope was to jump into the sea and try to reach the shore about 10 kilometres away.

◁ Fire at sea is something all sailors fear, even today. In Columbus's time, once a fire had started in the wooden ships, with their huge canvas sails, it was almost impossible to put out. Columbus was very lucky to survive. He was a strong swimmer but, more importantly, he found an oar floating in the sea. He was able to cling to it to keep himself afloat when he rested on his long swim to safety.

Columbus Arrives in Lisbon

◁ We know from his own diaries that Columbus was fascinated by old maps and charts, showing the continents and their coasts, the oceans and their currents. There is a story that Columbus and his brother, who had also come to settle in Lisbon, opened a business selling maps and books about travel and exploration. But, sadly, we do not know if the story is true.

In the fifteenth and sixteenth centuries Portugal and Spain both had powerful navies. There was a great deal of rivalry between the rulers of the two countries over whose navy was the most successful in discovering new territories. Prince Henry, one of the sons of King John I of Portugal, was known as 'Prince Henry the Navigator' because of his interest in exploration and support for explorers.

W EAK AND EXHAUSTED, COLUMBUS WAS washed up on a beach. He was lucky to have survived, many from his ship were drowned. Eventually he reached Lisbon, the capital of Portugal, and a great Atlantic seaport.

In Lisbon, Columbus found work acting as an agent for wealthy merchants. He travelled on Portuguese ships to distant destinations. He sailed northward to England and perhaps as far as Iceland. He also journeyed southward to Guinea, on the west coast of Africa, in search of gold and other treasures.

While Columbus was living in Lisbon he married Felipa Moniz Perestrello, a Portuguese noblewoman. Her father had been a fine sailor and she gave Columbus all his old maps.

Columbus and Felipa lived for a time on one of the Canary Islands, far out in the Atlantic Ocean. Living there, Columbus could study winds and tides very different from those he knew around the coasts of Italy and Portugal. He probably also heard the local sailors talking of the sights they saw and the strange islands glimpsed in the distant west, where the sun sank into the sea.

Sailing West to Reach the East

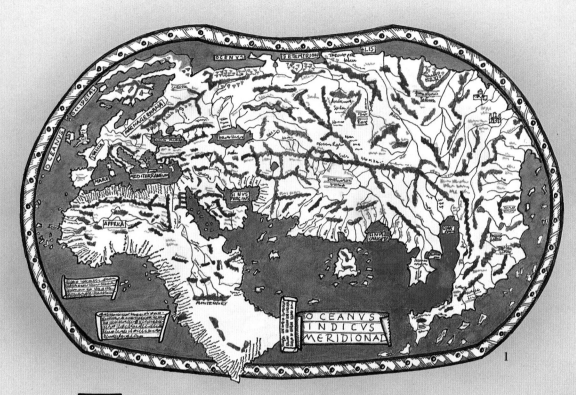

1

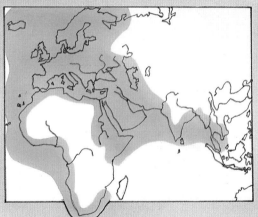

2

TOWARDS THE END OF THE fifteenth century there was a tremendous upsurge of enthusiasm for learning about the world. Everyone seemed to be interested, not just scholars. Works on geography, history and mathematics by earlier Greek, Roman, Jewish and Christian authors were translated. One that really captured people's imaginations was Marco Polo's account of his travels to the Far East about 200 years earlier. He had travelled overland and his journey had been full of dangers. The merchants and traders of Europe believed there must be an easier route to the riches of the east. And, since the Turks had closed the land routes, the obvious way was by sea.

1. Map of the world drawn in 1490 by the German geographer Henry Martellus. He based the map on the work of Claudius Ptolemy, a scholar who lived in Egypt in the second century AD. The coasts of the countries around the Mediterranean, north-west Europe and the west coast of Africa are quite recognizable and quite accurate.
2. The area shaded pink shows the area of Martellus's map.

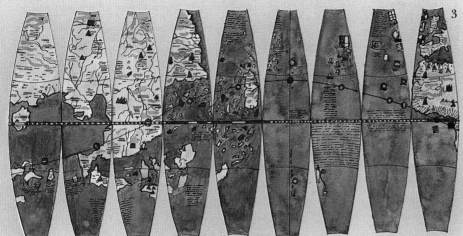

Traditionally, people had believed the earth to be flat. However, by Columbus's time most scholars had rejected this theory. They believed that the earth was shaped like a sphere. If this theory was correct, argued Columbus and a growing number of scholars, it would therefore be possible to reach the east by sailing west!

3. It is very difficult to show something three-dimensional, like the earth, on a flat sheet of paper. The geographer Martin Belrain got over the problem like this. His map also showed that sailing west to reach the east was perfectly possible.

4. The diagram shows the routes taken by Columbus on each of his four voyages from Spain to the New World. He left for the first voyage (black line) on 3 August in 1492 and returned in triumph on 15 March 1493. In September that year he left the port of Cadiz with a fleet of 17 ships (green line), returning in 1496. His third voyage (blue line) lasted from 1498 to 1500. On his fourth and last voyage (red line) Columbus reached the mainland of the American continent for the first time.

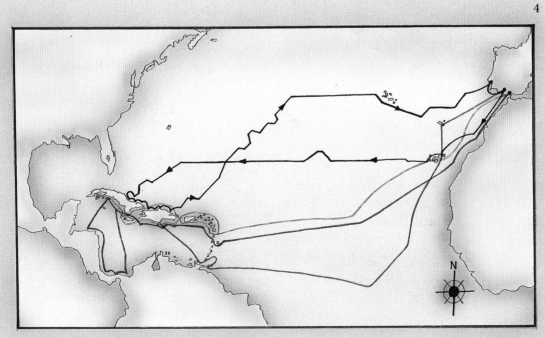

Finding the Money

COLUMBUS WAS NOT THE FIRST person to think that sailing west was the best way to reach the rich trading countries of the east. An Italian, Paolo Toscanelli, had put forward the idea several years earlier. Columbus, however, was the first person to want to put the theory to a practical test. But he needed money. Like other explorers he needed a patron, a rich person to pay for the cost of a ship, equipment, provisions and a crew.

No-one in Portugal was interested in his scheme, so, in 1485, Columbus moved to Palos, a busy Spanish port. Spain and Portugal were great rivals, each trying to discover more new territory than the other. So Columbus hoped that the Spanish would help him because the Portuguese had not.

After months of frustration and waiting, Columbus got the chance to explain his plans to King Ferdinand and Queen Isabella, the rulers of Spain. They listened politely, and Isabella even seemed interested. But the two rulers were more concerned with their war against the Moors. These were Arab Muslims whose ancestors had conquered southern Spain 700 years earlier. They did not have the time or the money to become Columbus's patrons.

▷ King Ferdinand and Queen Isabella were two of the most powerful rulers in Europe in Columbus's time. It was, therefore, a very great honour for Columbus that they agreed to receive him and hear his ideas about a new trade route to the east. During the meeting everyone stood except the king and queen. This was the custom for many centuries. Even today, at royal banquets, no-one is supposed to sit down before the members of royalty. In countries with a president the same rule applies.

Sailing Into the Unknown

SIX YEARS LATER, IN 1491, Columbus was no nearer finding a patron and putting his ideas to the test. Then, suddenly, his luck changed. Columbus's friends had been busy at the Spanish court, trying to persuade Ferdinand and Isabella to change their minds. Isabella was very religious, so they suggested that Columbus might take missionaries to convert to Christianity the people living in the far-off lands. They also pointed out that the Portuguese had just discovered a new route to the east around the southern tip of Africa, and might soon take over all the profitable trade with the east.

Ferdinand and Isabella were impressed, but it was their victory over the Moors early in 1492 that finally made them change their minds. Now they had money to spend on projects other than war. They summoned Columbus to court, and, after some arguments about the details of their agreement, appointed him to be Admiral of the Ocean Sea. They arranged for him to buy ships and provisions, and to recruit captains and crewmen from among the experienced seamen of Palos. Finally, on 3 August, 1492, Columbus set sail for the unknown in his ship the *Santa Maria*, followed by the *Pinta* and the *Nina*.

▽ Columbus was the driving force behind all his expeditions, particularly the first. No-one had done what he was setting out to do, so it was difficult to hire crews, even when he had the support of Ferdinand and Isabella. Another problem was that he was not a trained sailor or ship's captain. At last, he persuaded two captains, Martin Alonso Pinzon and Vincente Yanez Pinzon to join him. After that it was easier to hire crews. Although it is Columbus's name that is linked with the voyage, without the Pinzons Columbus could not have got there – but without Columbus the Pinzons would not have gone!

17

Finding the Way

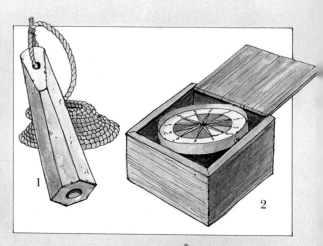

The *SANTA MARIA*, THE *PINTA* AND the *Nina*, the three ships that Columbus took on his first expedition, were all caravels. These were not the largest ships of the time, but they were light, fast and very easy to manoeuvre. They were ideal ships to use in unknown conditions: being light they sailed easily even if the winds were not strong; being fast they could make good progress across the ocean and being easy to manoeuvre they could get close to unfamiliar shores. Columbus used the *Santa Maria* as his flagship.

Columbus had few instruments to help him navigate his way into the unknown. Until his voyage westward, most expeditions had kept within sight of the coast they were exploring. Columbus had no such coast. All he had was a compass which showed the position of magnetic north, an astrolabe (see caption) and an hourglass to give a more accurate record of time than just watching the sun cross the sky each day. He also had a plumbline – a length of rope with a lead weight on the end – to measure the depth of coastal waters, to make sure the water was deep enough for the ship. Although there were some quite accurate maps and charts of Europe and the west coast of Africa, there was no map that could help Columbus. He really was 'sailing off the map'.

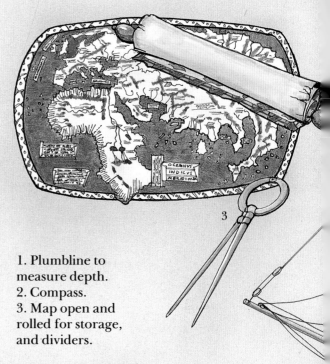

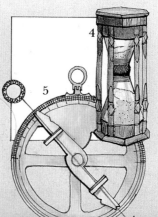

1. Plumbline to measure depth.
2. Compass.
3. Map open and rolled for storage, and dividers.

4. Hourglass to tell the time.
5. Astrolabe to measure the height of the sun and the stars above the horizon.

18

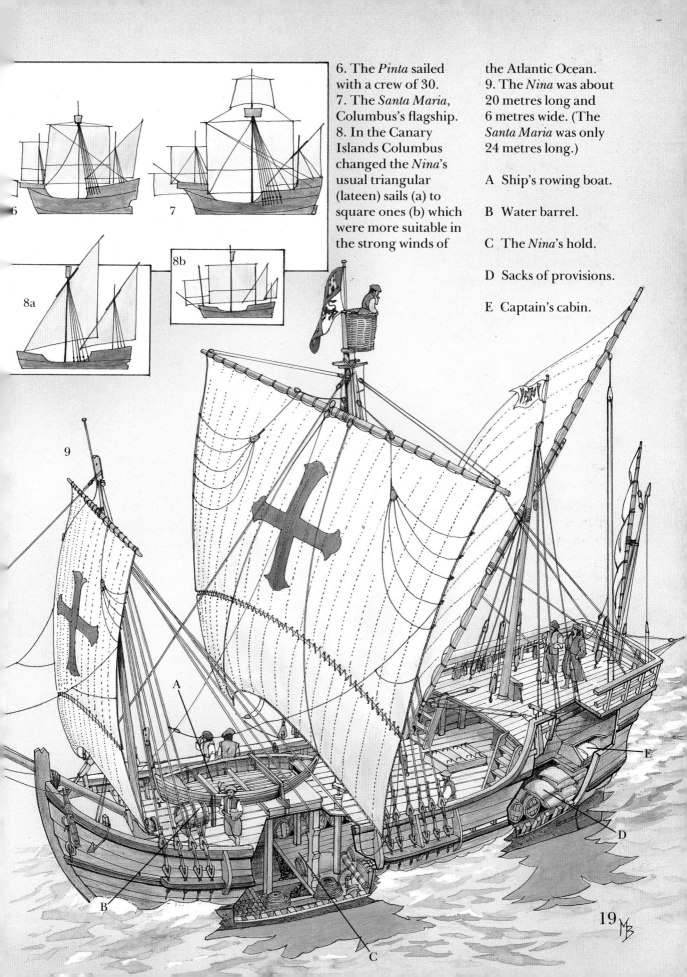

6. The *Pinta* sailed with a crew of 30.
7. The *Santa Maria*, Columbus's flagship.
8. In the Canary Islands Columbus changed the *Nina*'s usual triangular (lateen) sails (a) to square ones (b) which were more suitable in the strong winds of the Atlantic Ocean.
9. The *Nina* was about 20 metres long and 6 metres wide. (The *Santa Maria* was only 24 metres long.)

A Ship's rowing boat.

B Water barrel.

C The *Nina*'s hold.

D Sacks of provisions.

E Captain's cabin.

6

7

8a

8b

9

A

B

C

D

E

MB

Land at Last

AT FIRST, ALL WENT WELL. The weather was good and the ships were blown steadily westward by the winds known as Trade Winds. But after two weeks, the crews became restless. How long before they reached dry land? How long would the food and water last? They saw strange new sights: an enormous whale, an extraordinary mass of seaweed through which they sailed for days.

After three weeks, Columbus and his captains feared the crews would mutiny. Everyone, except Columbus, was angry and anxious. Then, at 2 am on 12 October, they saw white sand and black rocks glinting in the moonlight – land!

For the next few weeks Columbus sailed along this new coast, in search of the mainland he believed he would find. The local people were friendly. Columbus exchanged trinkets he had brought from Spain for gold and local produce. But where were the cities roofed with gold that he had read about? Where were the riches of the east?

Then, on Christmas night 1492, a real disaster struck the expedition. Columbus's ship, the *Santa Maria*, hit some rocks and sank.

▷ News of the wreck soon reached Guacanagari, the local chief. He sent men and boats to help the Spaniards unload what they could from the wreck and take it ashore. He also provided food, water and fire to warm the shivering sailors. He even sent his brothers to make sure that nothing was stolen. 'Not even so much as a piece of string was missing,' wrote Columbus in his diary.

△ The land
Columbus first saw
was San Salvador,
part of the chain of
islands now called the
Bahamas. He sailed
on to Cuba and
Hispaniola (modern
Haiti) where the *Santa
Maria* was wrecked. It
was lucky the wreck
was close to the shore,
so a lot of equipment
could be salvaged.

21

A Whole New World

To Columbus and his men, this new land was quite amazing, full of strange people, plants and animals. At the same time, to the local people, the Spaniards seemed equally strange. The three caravels towered above their canoes and were promptly called 'the houses on the water'.

At first everything went well between the locals and the newcomers. Sadly, this did not last. The Europeans were greedy and brutal. Columbus, sensing the chance to gain glory for Spain, and himself, was determined to use this new land and its people to win wealth and power. Although Guacanagari and his people had helped the Spaniards when the *Santa Maria* sank, Columbus saw them as a useful way of making money: they would fetch good prices in Europe as slaves.

Later Spanish explorers did find huge quantities of gold and silver in the New World, just as Columbus had dreamed. For Europe, however, the real and most lasting riches from the New World were its animals and, particularly, its plants. The pictures opposite show some of the plants that eventually reached Europe from what later explorers realized was a whole new continent. Columbus, to his dying day, remained certain that he had reached the fabled, wealthy east.

1. Turkey.
2. Making sugar loaves. Cane sugar was introduced to Spain by the Moors, but remained a luxury until it was taken to the New World in the seventeenth century. The conditions there were ideal for growing it in huge plantations. The cane syrup drips through a cloth bag, leaving behind the crystals which will form the sugar loaf.
3. Iguana.
4. Hammock woven from fibres from the agave plant's leaves.
5. Foot plough.

6. Sweet potato.
7. Tobacco.
8. Maize (sweetcorn).
9. Potato.
10. Tomato. Grown in southern Italy since the seventeenth century.
11. Beans
12. Pineapples also reached Europe in the seventeenth century.
13. Sunflower.
14. Chillies (centre) and sweet peppers.
15. Cocoa beans first reached Spain in 1520, but it was many years before chocolate was used as a sweet.
16. Marrow and gourd.
17. Agave. Fibres from the leaves were woven into cloth.
18. Prickly pear.

23

A Hero's Welcome

COLUMBUS AND HIS MEN DECIDED to build a camp using wood from the wrecked ship. Some of the men would stay there and continue to search for gold, while others returned to Spain with Columbus in the two remaining ships.

Columbus stayed until the camp was built. He asked Guacanagari, the chief of the local people, to protect it from more warlike local tribes. Then he and Martin Pinzon set sail for Europe. Columbus took with him some gold, some birds and animals, some cotton, herbs, amber and, most unkindly after all the help they had given him, some of the local people as prisoners.

The journey back was terrifying. There were violent storms and everyone thought they would die. Eventually, Columbus managed to steer his weatherbeaten ship into Lisbon harbour, and from there back home to Spain. Crowds flocked to greet him and to stare at the goods and people he had brought back with him. No-one, of course, had ever seen things like these before.

Ferdinand and Isabella summoned Columbus to court and received him with great honour. He was a hero.

▷ The return voyage was so bad that Columbus wrote an account of his discoveries and threw it overboard in a barrel, hoping that it would be found if he died at sea. But eventually he reached Spain and was able to tell his patrons, Ferdinand and Isabella, whose money had made the trip possible, all about his discoveries. It had been difficult to keep some of the plants alive on the voyage and much of the fruit had gone bad, but there was enough to prove the trip's success. Sadly, the local people Columbus had brought back were badly treated. Most of them became ill and died.

Columbus's Second Voyage

COLUMBUS HAD NO DIFFICULTY RAISING the money for a second voyage. He set off again in 1493 with a much larger expedition: 17 ships and 1200 men. This time he planned to conquer the whole territory, to build new cities and win glory and riches for Spain. He took seeds and grapevines to plant and animals for breeding. He took engineers to build mines for the gold he hoped to find and farmers to grow the crops. Several missionaries went too, to tell the local people about Christianity.

The crossing was good and the ships arrived safely. Everyone was looking forward to a reunion with the sailors who had remained behind at the camp. But as the ships approached the shore there were no signs of life.

Then, as Columbus and his men hurried ashore, they discovered the remains of two bodies on the beach. Then they realized that all the shelters had been pulled down and set on fire. Every man they had left behind was dead.

What had happened? It seems that the sailors had quarrelled with the local people. The sailors had been rough and greedy, stealing food and treasures and women, and threatening to shoot anyone who resisted them. So it was not surprising that Guacanagari's villagers, and other, fiercer local people, had attacked the Spaniards in self-defence.

The destruction of the camp and the deaths of the men he had left behind was a great blow to Columbus and the second expedition. He later learnt that Guacanagari had tried to warn the sailors that their behaviour would lead to trouble, but they had ignored his advice. Canabo, a very warlike local leader, accused Guacanagari of helping the Spaniards against his own people. So Guacanagari retreated to his village and Canabo and other warlike groups attacked the camp, burnt the shelters and killed the men who had been mistreating them.

Disgrace

THE DESTRUCTION OF THE CAMP was a bad sign. The second voyage was not a success. The site Columbus chose for the new settlement was damp and unhealthy and many of the settlers became ill. Food, too, was scarce. Although Columbus remained confident that he would find gold and the new colony would be successful, others were not so sure. His proud and cruel manner was also beginning to make him enemies.

After another trip exploring the coast, Columbus's crew rebelled. They were frightened and badly treated. Some fled and sailed for Spain, swiftly followed by Columbus.

Back in Spain Ferdinand and Isabella greeted Columbus coldly. They were particularly angry at reports that he had been selling the local people to Europe as slaves.

Two years later, they allowed him to return to the new lands. After exploring islands off the coast of modern Venezuela, he returned to the settlement. There, his harshness soon caused another rebellion among the settlers. When Ferdinand and Isabella heard this they sent Franciso de Bobadillo, a senior official, to run the colony. Furious, Columbus tried to resist. It was useless. He was arrested and sent back to Spain – a prisoner in chains.

◁ Columbus was a
very proud man, so
being sent back to
Spain in chains must
have been the most
awful disgrace. No
longer was he telling
everyone what to do,
he had to do what he
was told. As King
Ferdinand remarked:
'Columbus is a good
admiral, but he is a
bad governor.' All the
way back to Spain he
grumbled defiantly
'these chains have
been put on me by
royal command, I will
not have them
removed until I have
their majesties'
permission.' Even on
shore he dragged the
chains noisily behind
him everywhere he
went. He was bitter at
the way he had been
treated and this was
his way of protesting.

The Final Voyage

IN DECEMBER 1500 FERDINAND AND ISABELLA dismissed Columbus from his position as governor of the new lands. Columbus was angry because they seemed to listen to everyone's version of events except his own.

In 1502, however, they relented and let him sail west again. But now they encouraged other explorers to sail there too.

Columbus set out on his fourth voyage in 1502. This time, he explored the coast of modern Honduras, without realizing that he was on the mainland of a new continent. He found some gold, and spent months looking for more. Then disaster struck. His party was attacked and many were killed.

Although Columbus and some of his crew escaped, they were marooned for weeks before help arrived. Exhausted and ill, Columbus returned to Spain in 1504. He died two years later.

Today it is hard to imagine just how great Columbus's achievement was. No-one had travelled so far west before. No-one had been out of sight of land for so long. No-one knew for sure if there was anything, or nothing, beyond the sea's horizon. The only way to find out was to go. And that is what Columbus did.

▷ Columbus died in 1506, a bitter, angry man. His funeral was not the great state occasion for which he had once hoped. He was buried in a small monastery by the sea in Cadiz, ignored by the king and queen and all the people who had called him a hero only a few years earlier. But no-one can ignore the fact that it was Columbus who proved it was possible to sail the Atlantic.

Important Dates

1451 Christopher Columbus is born in Genoa, Italy
1453 Constantinople captured by the Turks
1474 or 1475 Columbus goes to Chios
1488 Bartholomew Dias rounds southern tip of Africa
1491 Columbus explains his ideas to King Ferdinand and Queen Isabella of Spain
1492 The Spanish army finally drives the Moors from Spain
1492 3 August Columbus leaves on his first voyage
1493 15 March Columbus returns September He sets out on his second voyage
1496 Columbus returns from his second voyage
1498 He sails on his third voyage
1500 Columbus is brought back to Spain in disgrace
1502 Columbus leaves on his final voyage and reaches the mainland of America
1504 He returns from his last voyage
1506 Columbus dies

Index